# Life Lines Volume II

برای عمه ی عزیزم با بهترین آرزوها

امیر علی

# Life Lines Volume II

Amir Ali Siassi

Library of Congress Control Number:     2009903803
ISBN:          Hardcover               978-1-4415-2979-4
               Softcover               978-1-4415-2978-7

**To order additional copies of this book, contact:**
Xlibris Corporation
1-888-795-4274
www.Xlibris.com
Orders@Xlibris.com
62099

# CONTENTS

Starting from now, here today and forward towards tomorrows, help us to increase peace for ease to show the power of our Love so that we may create a masterpiece of art—our own life. To your Presence, O Creator, we give you all of our gratitude and good attitudes for you have given us the gift of Life and the present of the moment.

# Prayer wit' no beginnin' and end

The highest form of prayer is thought control

Therefore, think only good and righteous thoughts, O Sole

even in moments of darkness see only perfection,

express only gratefulness, then choose your next reflection

In this process is found tranquility, peace and happiness

Know the song of the soul may be sung in many ways

and the sound of silence may be heard many times

for all of life's a meditation and we're contemplating the Divine

This is called true wakefulness or right-mindfullness

experienced like so everything in life is blessed

Those who attain choose to name it perfection

They use life and all its events as a meditation

# The Process of Creation

Most people really believe if they "have" a thing

like more money, time, love or any other thing

only then can they "do" a thing

like work at a job, take up a hobby, or undertake a relationship

which will finally allow them to "Be" a thing

happy, peaceful, conscious, or loving

Actually, in the Universe the reverse is true showing

it begins with "Being" the thing called happy, knowing

then you start "doing" things from this place of being

soon you'll find your doings are bringing in the things you're "having"

In life you don't have to "do" anything

it's all a question of what you're "Being"

to get, lets set into motion the process of creating

# Physics discovers Awareness

Physics was the first discipline of modern science

filled with concepts of spirits invading bodies was medicine

and astronomy was indistinguishable from astrology

Aristotle found modern physics with his inquiry into the ultimate nature of reality

Things were made of smaller things that were made of smaller things

and smaller things led him to the atom then the smallest named thing

Physics led the other sciences that dealt with some aspect of reality

and physics concerns itself with the core being of that reality

Chemistry without physics is inconceivable

Biology without chemistry is incomprehensible

Medicine, genetics, farming without biology are unimaginable

Growing out of the study of physics is the core of the scientific model

The discoveries of physics are showing our connection

to the rest of the Universe more so than our cultures direction

Physics implies that Consciousness brings the Universe into existence

and this Consciousness isn't in any one place concentrated

an interpretation is that the Universe is only made of Consciousness

# Being=God

Physical science informs us that the whole
creation is built up of multiple layers of energy
The subtlest is at the innermost stratum of creation
and builds up around itself different qualities, so it's growing
Recent discoveries of physics indicate the existence
of various types of elementary particles lying at the basis of all creation
The family of elementary particles is found to be increasing
showing creation exists in innumerable strata of energy
Fine particles give rise to neutrons and protons
which build up into the nucleus of an atom, which in turn build to atoms
The atoms comprise of molecules and the molecules make up
the different forms of phenomena and constitute the entire visible universe
This is how physics is discovering finer layers of creation
Then when the atom was split, investigations into the nucleus gave
rise to nuclear physics
Investigations into the field of electrons gave rise to electronics
and as our knowledge of the finer fields of creation is increasing
it is enabling us to be more powerful in life
Underneath the subtlest layer of all that exists in the relative field
is the abstract, absolute field of pure Being or Existence
which is unmanifested and transcendental, it's neither matter nor energy
This state of pure existence underlies all that exists
everything is the expression of this pure existence or absolute being
which is the essential constituent of all relative life
The one eternal unmanifested absolute Being manifests
itself in many forms of lives and existences in creation

# L-O-V-E=U

Real love is unlimiting

no beginning, and no ending

It always was, is, and will be

real love's the always reality

Unlimited and always means free

real love is that which is really free

Freely unlimiting translates into eternality

at the deepest, highest, widest place of being

you will come to know that U are L-O-V-E

and through it's expression we're seeking

to know and experience our real being

# O Good God

My God loves no one more than any other

so don't believe in the God who loves some more than others

these are what I call fictitious religions

and they're also blasphemies and sacrileges

Yo don't bastardize the word of the Lord in order to justify

your fears and rationalize your insane treatment of life

You'll say all about the false God to continue limiting each other

hurting each other, in God's name you're killing each other

You've invoked the Lord's name, waved unholy flags

carried crosses for centuries in battlefields on your backs

as proof that God loves some more than others

and would ask you to kill to prove it to yourselves and others

I tell you God's love is unconditional and unlimited

if you accept this statement of God's all inclusiveness

it will destroy the way you've constructed marriages institution

it'll destroy all your religions and governmental institutions

For you've created a culture based on exclusion

supported by a cultural myth of a God who is exclusive

but the culture of God is based on inclusion

In God's love any and everyone is included

Into the King's kingdom any and everyone is invited

So know there's no place to go just be here and now's the only time

# Love Everyone Unconditionally

When we begin to increase the number of people

for whom unconditional love we feel

we become aware of the many security, sensation

and power dramas that each of them are playin'

we realize that we don't have enough energy and time

with a "bleeding heart" to respond to the problems in their life

Our life works best when we love, serve and flow positivity

from the consciousness that the Universe gave this energy

and it feels wonderful to pass along this energy

As we become more conscious, increasing is our energy

and less of it will be drained by our own security,

sensation and power addictions

Then we will liberate a continuous stream

that will flow into loving yourself

and serving people around yourself

# Love & Attachment

Due to the subtle fear of freedom
everyone wants to be a slave
Of course we all talk about freedom
but to be really free we need to be brave
because when you are really free you're alone
If you are courageous enough to be alone only then can you be free
and very few are brave enough to be alone
for the great majority need someone to not feel lonely
so they occupy themselves with others to not get bored with themselves
since we can't live for ourselves, we live for others
the same is the case with the someone else
he or she can't live alone, hence the search for the other
Since they are searching for attachment, commitment, bondage
sooner rather than later they will get married
then the two persons to each other become slaves
next they start struggling to become free
Usually whatsoever we get, we get bored with
and whatsoever we don't get, becomes an obsession
Real Love can't and doesn't become attachment
the mechanism for love to turn into attachment is possession
We must remain individuals and be independent
we can come together, unite, but no one possesses
then there'll be no bondage and no attachment
when we know who this being is which is in us
and what this consciousness is which is us, we'll not be attached
only then can one really love
while sharing with no conditions and expectations
we overflow, in this overflowing of ourselves is love

# Fear of Love turns into Hate

A person who has suppressed sex

will always be afraid of love

because once love comes so does sex

Sex is of the body and the sole is love

so love cannot be allowed to happen

because then sex will come next

that person's loving hand can happen

to turn into a touch of sex

Hence fear arises out of the instinct repressed

and instead of love that person will be filled with hatred

Since any energy that's repressed

reverses itself and goes to its original nature

# The Alchemy of Love

A miracle happens when you accept a truth

the very acceptance changes you

When you become true to yourself, then you're not afraid of fear

if you're not afraid to accept your fear, it'll start to disappear

With fear we don't know what to do

neither do others know what to do

For there is nothing to be done

but the moment we stop pretending, we become one

or real, and this fearlessness to accept truth

rather than hide behind lies changes you

into a true, authentic, genuine being

fearless we become that which we were: loving

# The Strength of Goodness

One's who go Away are always the best

those who resist and assert themselves are the best

Those mediocre yield, yea sayers don't rebel

However, the more intelligent minds do rebel

They don't need to follow, they can stand alone

Ones who seem to be good are weak and lonely

Goodness must come out of an overflowing floodlike strength

like more lively and righteous are sinners who become saints

for now no power can interrupt to corrupt them

because their goodness stems and is rooted in strength

# Peaceful Purpose

To thrive and be alive the human spirit

needs to be permitted to do its natural living

it needs to be present in its surroundings

tuned in to the time and place of Here, Now

To touch the well-spring of the creative sole

it has to act on what it knows to be possible

and it needs to experience how its actions affect the universe

People get the sensation of personal power as that happens

I perceive, I believe leads me

to conceive and achieve deeds

knowing to do the right thing

is showing the right thing to do, growing

from the presence's essence present

in each moment and every second

so our deepest wishes and hopes do surface

for most of us are seeking peace and its purpose

# Quality's more than Quantity

You know when we do our best

we are gonna live life very intense

which will be filled with positivity & productivity

giving ourselves to our family and community

It's the action that makes us feel joyous

Doing our best is acting for and from the joy of it

not because we're expecting a reward

Most people only take action when they expect a reward

and that takes away from the joy of the action

That's the reason they don't do their best in their actions

# Nice & Slow with NowHere to go

Innocent people are always without time-consciousness

there is no rush or hurry to go anywhere for they're in the moments

they are tasting each moment

savoring the flavor of every moment

but the majority are in the past or future, hence they miss this very moment

The future is a mystery, the past is history, the only time is now!

The future is yet to be, the past is no more, so all is now

Hey if we can slow down a little play like children here and now

then these techniques can work miracles being here and now

But in this century we've become too time-conscious

it's difficult here for nowhere are they teaching innocence

and now everywhere they are teaching cleverness

Universities don't make us innocent rather they teach cleverness

The more clever you are the readier you'll be in the competitive world

the more innocent you are the steadier you'll be in samadhi's world

And unfortunately the majority have chosen this world to be the goal

# Spontaneous Activity Charges

When we relax become passive we feel something is lost

remain with that passivity allow this thing to be lost

A balancing point will come when we'll be freer

we'll be right at the point of no anxious fever

we will be simply our self, not pushed into activity

or pulled by someone else into activity

Now activity will start happening through us

but it will be spontaneous and natural to us

When the activity is spontaneous we won't feel any tension through it

we won't feel any burden, but we'll thoroughly enjoy it

The activity will be an end unto itself

it will not be a means to reach somewhere else

it'll be just an overflow of our own energy

Since this overflow will be the presence's energy

Whatsoever we're doing will become absolute in itself

and after it we won't be tired rather we'll feel refreshed

Know that a feverish activity tires us for it is ill

Whereas, a natural activity charges us, after it we're more vital

# Alertness Transforms Energy

For example when anger comes

look at it, observe it, of 'it' be conscious

and the more alert you are the less anger

The moment you're alertness, there is no anger

because energy is neutral, in action

when alertness is the reaction

the same energy which is anger becomes compassion

since energy is one these are all expressions

energy can become moods in basic situations

The alertness, awareness moves the energy in more positive, productive planes

That's why Buddha said, "Whatsoever you do, do it with a conscious mind state."

# Awareness Overcomes Anxiety

Fight or flight mode when you feel fright

Just as the fear enters be alert and it goes

For you can only be afraid when you lose alertness

A brave person in moments of fear bring their alertness

And a coward is one who hasn't empowered their alertness

When you're tense and anxiety-ridden

Tap into your awareness and quit thinking

Since anxiety can't be solved by thinking

Thinking itself is a sort of anxiety, giving

More thought is like adding fuel to the fire

So if you desire to overcome it you must be aware

# Don't IDentify with Actions to Become free

Our actions are very irrelevant to our Being

That is exactly why a person of understanding

works, does a thousand and one things

but knows it would be unreal, untrue to be identifying

When he goes to the office he may be a president

but then the moment he leaves the office he's no longer a president

he comes home to a wife and child, he becomes a husband and father

if he has a sister or brother he becomes a brother

the times he nourishes or nurtures he has the features of a mother

still his being keeps free of all these, he's the other

the other is being or god remaining beyond

In fact the less we identify, the freer we become

# From the Outer to the Inner

From the outer we enter the inner

but the outer can't change the inner

the outer can help or it can hinder

remember outer change isn't of the inner

We change bodies for lives and still are unsatisfied

for we're only content when the inner sole crystallizes

so don't let your sole be possessed and mind obsessed with the outer

for then you're escaping and postpone changing the inner

don't forget this: it is the inner that's central which remains eternal

so let the outer help complement the kernel

also know the outer in relation to the inner is part and parcel

Yo, it's through the periphery or circumference that we enter the sole

only give the boundary as much attention and significance

for the center of the circle or home to be of utmost importance

# Essence at Ease

The key is for the essence to be at ease

whatever we're doing, at our core or deepness

remain centered, calm and at ease

Then we can be anywhere and remain unpolluted

our purity will remain, we can keep our innocence

The essence is at ease is the quality we have to bring

into each and every act we are doing

so much so that it permeates, pervades our existence

and then we will retain the quality of all meditations

# The Source

I love you, the natural feeling is you are the source

that is not really so for I am the source

and you are just a screen on which I project my love

I project my love on you and say you are the source of my love

This is not a fact rather it is a fiction

that which is the source and projections distinction

My love energy projected onto you makes you lovely

to someone else you may not be so lovely

If you are or become the source of love

then toward you everyone will feel love

# I Am No-thing

Awareness in No-thing transcends features of the creature

and from all things visible, we become No-thing to what is Nature &
Creature

then we are in that Eternal One, Creator or God

and shall feel within the highest virtue of Love

the treasure beyond measure for the sole

is where it goes from the Somewhat into that No-thingness whole

The sole here can do nothing and is no-thing

other than an image of Being and only the Lord is to me

I solely only give glory to the Eternal One Being

and will nothing of myself that so God may will all in me

being unto me my God, Maker, Creator and all things

# NoBody

Hu's callin' me out

NoBody 'cause I'm all out

The flawless, lawless sole

No system of late has the wisdom to control

That's Y we Rage Against the Machine

Because we crave in so many ways to get free

From the mental chains & shackles of society

To change its shape, stay fit and maintain sobriety

With this as the main aim of our mindframe

Be more humane to win in life's game

Yo I don't like pain but I love pleasure

So I know I will abstain from causin' pressure

If I gotta go against the grain to gain the lost treasure

I will kill the ill to heal be real and become better

Indivisible-Invincible-Individuals, Indivisible-Invincible-Individuals

My mystical spiritual rituals are to be unseen, invisible

Like HichKas which has the definition of NoBody in person

# Holy Ghost

The Holy Ghost always guides us as a duty

know our joy to be his fully and truly

His Will is joy for each and everyone

Speaking for the kingdom of God

Therefore, following Him is the easiest thing in the world

being the only thing that's easy since it's not of the world

Everything in the world perceives orders of difficulty

due to the ego perceiving nothing as desirable wholly

By proving to ourselves there is no order of difficulty in miracles

We'll convince ourselves that in a state that's natural

there's only ease because it's a state of grace

and the natural state of human beings is grace

Not being in the state of grace everything we do becomes a strain

because we were not created for the environment we've made

We are happy only when we know we're with God

there we will experience ease for that's where we belong

It's also the only environment that is worthy of Him

because beyond anything he can make is the worth of Him

# Holy Relationships

when each one looks wholly within

and has seen nothing missin'

then we accept our completion

extend it with others by joinin'

between these selves seeing no difference

knowing differences are only of the body

not denying the truth because it's reality

and through this we attain relationships so holy

these kinds of relationships are heavenly

this type of communion is teaching

in differences do not be believing

faith in sameness gives sight to division vision

reason now leads us to the logical conclusion of union

it must reach out of the body for soles to combine

just so that sameness which lies beneath them all actualizes

# Highly Evolved Societies

Highly Evolved Beings do the daily tasks or jobs

that must be done for a society to exist and function

they're the most highly rewarded workers in the service of All

and this to a highly evolved being isn't considered work at all

but the highest form of self-fulfillment, the ideas and experiences

humans have created around self-expression

are simply not part of the highly evolved beings culture

to them success' definition is foreign for there is no failure

Their experience of accomplishments or achievements

comes from understanding what real value is and it's appreciation

"Achieving" is defined as doing what brings value

the highly evolved beings do have a system of values

they value that which produces benefit to All

We see greater benefit in games played with balls

than in leading offspring to remember life's greatest significances

or sourcing members of society's necessary spiritual sustenance

Highly Evolved Beings honor those who minister or teach

because it's what works and that's of value for society

In a highly evolved society there are no have-nots

because they apply two basic essential principles, One

we are All One and Two there is enough for All Beings

They are conscious of the interrelatedness of all things

so none of the natural resources are destroyed or wasted

on a Highly Evolved Beings home planet

# Higher Learning

In a Highly Evolved Being society there's no such thing as a "school system"

offspring are reminded what's so and what works as their process of education

Offspring aren't raised by parents but by their elders

though they aren't necessarily separated from their parents

who may be with them whenever they wish

and spend as much time with them as they like

What we call school is translated as "learning time"

Offspring choose the skills they would like to acquire

as opposed to being pressured to learn what others require

Intrinsic Motivation is thus at its highest level or peak

and so skills are gained quickly with joy and ease

They have a Triangular Code of Awareness, Honesty, Responsibility

this isn't something that is forced into the Highly Evolved Being

rather it's received almost by osmosis

through behaviors modeled by adults for kids

because in Highly Evolved Cultures adults are knowing

that their children do what they see others are showing

The main difference between a Highly Evolved Being Society

is that they have truthful observation as opposed to human societies

where many deny what they see or don't do what serves them

Ample samples of failures to change the masses behaviors by religions

For another example more to oppress than to assist do governments

Furthermore we have health-care that's more like a disease-care system

spending one-tenth on preventing diseases and nine-tenth on managing them

and then deny that profit motive is what stops any real progress

on educating people on how to act, eat, and live in optimal health and success

# EDucation

Humans are born as a potentiality

We are not born as an actuality

This is very special and extraordinary

The animals are all born perfect instinctively

Humans are the only imperfect animal

Thus growth and evolution are possible

Education is the bridge between our potential and the actual

Education isn't being done in universities, colleges, and schools

They only prepare you to get a good job and a sum of some outcome

Maybe give us a better living standard not a better standard of life, they're not synonomous

The so-called education prepares us to earn bread in the world

And Jesus says, "Man cannot live on bread alone."

Real education is to give us outer and inner wealth

Right education is to bring us more health

True education teaches you to be yourself

Education means to make actual that which is potential

# Getting to Purpose in Life

Begins by going within and discovering that purpose

is about unconditional love and being of service

and making contact with what is here about us always

can and does alter our worldview in many ways

Suffering decreases because the emphasis isn't "why me?"

knowing you're experiencing that which is necessary

even if you don't understand then what's going on

nevertheless you still go on with it

Enlightenment can be defined as the quiet acceptance of what is

or the state of "lightening up"

no hostility, anger or remorse nor judgement

only a willingness to go with it and not fight it

Going beyond outcome in life about what's in it for you, you become unconcerned

attitudes and behaviors focus more so on the fulfillment of your purpose

transcending success, achievement and performance

as indications of your holy life's mission

living fully lovingly in the moment

for the presents of the presence gaining admission

# Life's 2 Balances

On Life's scale there are 2 balances

One is of being and the other of doing

Your being or nature is already the case

While doing is not already the case

True to survive we had to achieve and do much

But our activity can lead us away from our being

That whatever you have or can do is not "you"

For your being precedes and succeeds all you have or can do

Your activity or achieving is the circumference or outer

Whereas your being is you, your center and inner

# Life's Dialectical

Life lives through opposition, challenge creates energy

And life moves through it, releasing energy

Hegelians call this a dialectical movement, thesis

Antithesis and then the synthesis again becomes a thesis

that makes its own antithesis which is continuous

You know life's not logical or monotonous

Logic can't tolerate the contradictory

Since it has to explain that life isn't contradictory

Logical is science and math, therefore they're not totally true to life

Using the apparently opposite but deep down complimentary is life

Life is possible only because of the opposites

Woman and man are the basic opposition

Then the challenge creates the phenomenon of love

And all of life moves around love

Lover's go away from each other become polar opposites

They move to the farthest corner possible

Then again in the evening they're making love

Getting attracted when they're simply man and woman, not lovers

But the moment they become one again

Is the moment they've started being separate again

Therefore life creates energy through polarities

Life cannot exist without any polarities

If two lovers really become one they disappear from life

They're liberated freed from having to come back to life

Because they've achieved non-duality

Meaning they've reached lasting unity

# Life's A Celebration

Society keeps preaching that use is life's goal

I am saying this use is not life's goal

Live in society to it be useful

but remain capable of being useless

retained must be this capacity

otherwise instead of being a person you become a thing

Remember use is for society

society uses its members and members use society

Life is not for use, it is non-utilitarian

Life is a play, it's a celebration

So simply enjoy the joy of the eternal now

Being here is the nearest, clearest route

# Wide Life

They got cupid with stupid twisted

Then called a mystic a misfit

Next labeled an angelic rebel

A revolutionary devil

tried to make a family man an outcast

I sided with the Maker to outlast

And decided to take the route that

Leads to getting freer, lighter I'M all about that

Fly feeling, high life living

Giving my rhymes more meaning

Seeing or hearing the one being

Readying the ground, foundation reaching

Reaping official benefits known

Experiencing reality directly from the seeds sown

Gathering together creeds we own

To fathom causes effect and actions reaction

One comes to visions point of wisdom

From which joins the king to his kingdom

Hierarchy of beings becomes evident

How we've evolved becomes apparent

The past lives dissolve into parallel worlds

Yet unshown, but known to have grown from the sole

# In the road to Success

The road to success isn't straight.

There are loops called CONFUSION,

curves called FAILURES,

speed bumps known as FRIENDS,

red lights named ENEMIES,

caution lights known as FAMILY.

You'll have flats called JOBS,

but if your spare is DETERMINATION,

with an engine called PERSEVERANCE,

insurance FAITH and the driver being HOLINESS,

You will make it to a state called SUCCESS.

May that state praise your days and raise you in all ways

GOD BLESS your fate, solely, for a heavenly destiny!

# In(case) 4 Cause(in)

Amir 347 @ yahoo.com

I am (ear) all (eye) see for heaven

c**ALL** c**OM**e come calma c (**ALMA**)

Ya **HU** my cause (in) MICHEL

Who I am with (in) my (shell)  (U)

Who am i (with) out my (shell) I

I hope all is well with you, your familiar family

and wish well-wishers a well which swells with

the fountain of youth on the mountain of truth . . .

           (use)                         (truce)

               truly**yours** AA

2 My 1st cause[in] of D dozen out D oven . . . allofasuddin!!!

HAE, HI, HO gullable GUILLY

Mrs./Ms.\do you miss ME

I miserabley want WE 2 free willy

I still simply want 2 play silly

Tipsy Gipsy cum or lay pretty

yell o-r say hell-o fell-o yell-ow kitty

gecko's echo letgo O' e-g-O's!

N E Ways so Say what's Up?

Chick's or Hen's butts—WITCH!

but Which then Hells'den or Kids'hen

for (4) more sore poor Children who fell VicDim

2 (to) sink in this stinkin' thinkin' Life Of Sin

whY WE swim in a Pis-Pot of soggy shit


PisS . . . Potty is pissing Notty KNOWledge shitting Witty Wisdom

with his Expert Experience in Intuition

# Ouija Board

The Ouija Board was invented by William Fuld of Baltimore

It is approximately 15 inches wide and 22 inches long, for

the alphabet letters are printed in easy to read capital form

The word "yes" appears in the upper left-hand corner

and the word "no" is in the upper right-hand corner

Beneath the alphabet are the numbers from 1 to 9 plus a zero

At the very bottom of the board the word "goodby" is printed, also

a small pointer comes with the board

This pointer is like a three-legged miniature table of triangular form

Participants place their hands on the pointer, to operate the board

the pointer itself rests on the board

To become acquainted place hands on the pointer and run it lightly
across the board

when working properly, the pointer will move seemingly by itself
across the board

begin experimenting by asking questions, and/or

sitting silently with hands on the pointer to get a message from the
Ouija Board

# I Ching

The I Ching is also called the Book of Changes

It's a symbol system used to identify order in random events

The text describes an ancient system of cosmology and philosophy

that's intrinsic to ancient Chinese cultural beliefs

The cosmology centers on the ideas of the dynamic balance of opposites

acceptance of the inevitability of change and the evolution of events

as a process

I Ching has been used for more than 5,000 years as an aid to making

decisions

It's a long standing popular source of inspiration and wisdom

# AromaTherapy

Aromatherapy is the practice

of using volatile plant oils

including essential oils,

or a plants pure essence

for psychological, physical wellness

also uses other natural ingredients

such as vegetable oils cold pressed

jojoba, milk powders, hydrosols

sugars, clays, muds and sea salts

# Allopathy

In Greek, Allo means "opposite" and pathos means "suffering"

It's the system of medical practice which treats

dis-ease by the use of agents or remedies

which produce effects different from those of the dis-ease

The philosophy of Allopathy is the extreme opposite of Homeopathy

# Naturopathy

Is a system of treatment and therapy

That relies exclusively on natural remedies

such as sunlight, air, water, complimented by the ground

supplemented with diet and therapies like acupuncture and massage
all-around

It's based on the belief that the body is self-healing

that the body will repair itself and recover from ill-feeling

spontaneously if it is in a healthy environment

Naturopaths have many recommendations for creating a healthy
environment

They claim to be holistic, which means they believe the natural body

is joined to a supernatural soul and a nonphysical mind

and the three must be treated as a unit or combined

being fond of terms: "balance", "harmony", and "energy"

It's often rooted in mysticism and a metaphysical belief in "vitalism"

Or the doctrine that the phenomena of life cannot be described in purely
mechanical terms

because there is something immaterial which distinguishes living
from inanimate matter

# HydroTherapy

Hydrotherapy is the use of water

for health to be revitalized, maintained and restored

Treatments include saunas, steam baths, hot/cold showers

towel wraps and cold or hot water compresses

In hydrotherapy there's a physiological basis

Cold is stimulating causing superficial blood vessels to constrict

diverting the blood to internal organs

Hot water relaxes or calms

causes blood vessels to dilate

and from the body tissues removes waste

Alternating hot and cold water also improves elimination,

decreases inflammation and stimulates circulation

# Ayurveda

In Sanskrit Ayur means life and Veda means science

Ayurveda is an Indian system of traditional medicine

practiced in other parts of the world as alternative medicine

It's methods include the use of herbs, massage and yoga exercise

Ayurveda believes the five great elements

earth, water, fire, air and space form the universe

that semen, chyle, blood, fat, bone, marrow and flesh

are the body's seven primary constituent elements

It emphasizes a balance of three substances

bile, phlegm, and wind/spirit/air each representing divine forces

It believes that we possess a unique blend of these doshas

wind/spirit/air is vata, pitta is bile and phlegm is kapha

but that some have more vata, pitta, or kapha

# Massage's History

Massage is one of the earliest practices of humankind

Is also said to be the most natural and instinctive means of healing

5,000 years ago artifacts have been tracked in many countries

indicating that women and men massaged their muscles with herbs or oils

3000 BC records reveal that the Chinese used massage aka Amma

along with plant poultices and exercise for remedies, the modern term is Tui-na

1800 BC knowledge of massage comes to India from China

and becomes an important part of Hinduism, The Ayur-Veda

or Art of Life, a sacred book of the Hindus includes massage at the bath or Tshanpau

that consists of kneading extremities, tapotement, friction, cracking joints
and perfume anointment

300 BC The Greeks used massage in conjunction with bathing and gymnastics

From here is the Hippocratic oath's origins, which are still practiced

The Romans picked up bathing traditions from the Greeks

Massage was used on gymnasts of the day as a way to prevent disease

500 AD The Amma method, which originated in China enters Japan

and is initiated using similar points of stimulation

but is now familiar as Tsubo or finger pressure

points of acupressure are pressed to balance the circulation of fluids and Chi or Ki

1450-1600 In Europe the renaissance revives interest

in health practices, arts and sciences

1914-1918 Massage plays an important role during the 1st World War

in providing lymphatic drainage and rehabilitation for wounded soldiers

1939-1945 WW2 penicillin is first introduced and used on wounded soldiers

to physical therapy, massage assumes a secondary role

1960-present another massage renaissance begins to take place in the USA

A surge of interest in the practice and value of massage develops in the public,
professional & lay

With the increase in cost rates of traditional medicine, a way has opened
for alternatives

Today, more people experience the healing qualities of touch through the art
of Massage Therapy

# Mithra

Mithra or Mitra is also worshipped as Itu

in India and the homes of the Hindus

Mithra being the Sun-God

is believed to be a mediator between man and God

and between the Sky and Earth

It is said he was born on the 25th of December

Christians believe he was also born of a Virgin

Mithra was an esteemed chief God of the Persians

and that the Lamb is his symbol

He had twelve satellites or disciples

much like the amount of months in a years time

# MArí

"The Wonderful" Miria is of course, Mari

or Marian-Miriam-Mariamne, Mother Mary

In Witchcraft's Faery tradition she's the full moon aspect of the Goddess

The sense of wonder, joy and delight in the natural world is witchcraft's essence

Marian is the ancient pagan mermaid or Sea Goddess

Mariamne is also known as the ancient pagan Sea Lamb

She's the patroness of poets and lovers on the land

the proud mother of the Archer of Love is Mari

and the renowned mother of one of God's prophets is Mary

# The 4 Prototypes of Women

When women are searching

on the path of knowledge for meaning

these four classic prototypes can help them identify

One is not the sexual virgin but The Virgin is defined

as the person whose search comes from complete independence

and everything she gets alone is through taking on challenges

Next, The Martyr finds her way to self-knowledge

through pain, surrender, and suffering

The Saint finds her true reason for living

in unconditional love and in her ability to be giving

without asking for anything in return

And The Witch justifies her existence in turn

by going, searching for complete and limitless pleasure

# Born of the Virgin

One can be born again

twice-born aka rebirth

not out of two bodies or dualism

but virgin like through yourself

out of the One in all beings & things

First birth's from sex like everybody else

Second coming from inner unison

forming the state of being innocent

not God and Nature's gift of mother/father union

and now this blessing of innocence

can't be lost for there's nothing more to be gained

The moment we beings transcend existence

only then will things never ever change

That's when we've returned to Oneness

# Interpretation of Jesus' Crucifixion

To the Western state of mind

there is no rebirth, reincarnation or succession of lives

so the meaning of crucifixion they haven't deeply analyzed

They have a myth that Jesus suffered for us

that his suffering was a salvation for us

but this is not true to the facts, just

ask yourself this question why is humanity still suffering

If his crucifixion was a repentance for all our guilt and sin

then it was in vain for guilt, sin and suffering are continuing

The Eastern analysis has a different view

Christ's crucifixion happened because of karma that was due

this was his last life in physical form, he's not entering another body's womb

so he suffered for himself and for his past karmas

No one can suffer for anyone else we are a slave of our karmas

and the crucifixion closed his own account of karma

# The Messiah

There exists, persists this myth of an anticipated Messiah

Mohammad, Jesus, Moses, Buddha who was the messiah

These men transformed a few peoples' lives and living conditions,

but when The Messiah comes the planet will be transformed in a flash
of illumination

So then the ideal of the ultimate messiah is impossible

Or else somebody until now would've claimed it if it was possible

The Messiah is nothing but an awakening of the inside

It's a quality within which redeems, know it's not from the outside

# The True Guru

The Guru is the one towards whom you are gravitated

around whom you are pulled forward like a magnet

And there are people who have charisma

getting pulled toward them is no enigma

they may be or become great political leaders

the difference between a guru and charismatic leader

is when you're pulled towards a guru, you suddenly feel you're pulled inwards

if you're pulled towards a person who makes you a slave, then that is outwards

That person may have magnetic power: physical beauty, sheer vitality or great intelligence

but that person causes you to go away from yourself

and the closer you come to a guru the closer you come to yourself

You become more independent the more you're attracted towards a guru

You feel freer the more you become surrendered to a guru

if by surrendering you become more powerful, then you are near the guru

The being that pulls you towards him or herself just to throw you back to yourself is the guru

This is the criterion the whole effort has to be helping you to become yourself is the work of a guru

# A Master

A master is one who creates

a high level of similarity, or consistency, intentionally

A student creates consistency unintentionally

A person who always reacts the same way

to certain circumstances, for instance, often says:

"I couldn't help it" is not what a master would say

If a person gets commended or receives praise

and they respond with 'It was automatic, anybody would do it.'

A master is someone who would never, ever do this.

Therefore, a master is a person who literally

knows what she or he is doing and why

# Teachers & Masters

Teachers are many, Masters are very rare

You'll meet many Teachers, they're everywhere

they never demand on the contrary, they supply

Teachers give you info and knowledge, which can't satisfy

like talking about a lamp won't create light

that's why people go from teacher to teacher in search of light

When they come across a Master

there is a chance they'll miss the Master

because they come with expectations

and Masters never fulfill anybody's expectations

Our expectations come from our mind

for the Sole to be possible quiet the mind

free yourself from foolish desires and false expectations

The reason an enlightened Master never fulfills expectations

is for us to be more real, light and present

not stuck in the past or far out in the future, but be here in the moment

# The Rationalist and Atheist

We can't be both a rationalist and an atheist

A rationalist suspends all beliefs

A rationalist can only be an agnostic

They can only say "I don't know", the minute

They say "I know" they aren't rationalists

A rationalist will avoid all attempts of being dogmatic

They have to live without a philosophy or religion

Atheism means you're against theism

Theism or believing in God is a belief

Atheism or believing in no God is another belief

# Thoreau's Q's & A's

Q's: Can a being be a philosopher and not maintain

their vital heat by better methods than others?

The life humans praise or regard as successful is one game,

why should we exaggerate any one at the expense of the others?

If the civilized humans pursuits aren't worthier than the savages

if they're concerned with obtaining luxuries why should they live better than the former?

Why is it that humans give so poor an account of their days

if they have not been slumbering voyagers?

Why should we live with such hurry in life and waste it?

What do we want living close to us?

What separates an individual from his fellows and makes them solitary, where is that space?

A's: I never knew, and never will know a worse man than myself!

No method or discipline can supersede the necessity of being always aware!

The wise perceive that only great and worthy things have any absolute wealth!

We are still forced to cut our spiritual bread far thinner than our forefathers did their wheaten share!

We are determined to be starved before we are hungry! Well,

the fashions which the herd follow are set by the luxurious and dissipated!

All men want something to do, or rather something to be for help!

# Quest Curious

Curiosity is the pre-requisite

to beginning the journey of inquiry into existence

It's necessary as a start

but then one has to have more heart

One has to make life a quest

curiosity creates questions, then life doesn't become a quest

Remember questions are many, a quest is one

when some question has such significance to your life, then your quest has begun

Philosophy is curiosity, Religion is a quest for the truth

It wants to know from experience it's truth

and to have that quality is among the greatest blessings one can choose

# What is Eckankar?

Eckankar is a religious movement

which focuses on spiritual exercises

allowing practitioners to experience

what followers call the Light & Sound of God

Eckankar means co-worker with God

or Ik Onkar, a Sikh term from where it's name is gotten

One of the basic tenets is that soul (awareness, consciousness)

can travel freely in other planes of reality and leave the body in full consciousness

certain mantras are used to help spiritual development

and dreams are regarded as an important teaching instrument

Eck teaches that in one's lifetime it's possible to attain spiritual liberation,

it's possible to achieve the realization of oneself as soul or self-realization,

and the realization of oneself as a spark of God is God-realization

For all Eckists the final spiritual goal is to become conscious co-workers with God

# The Essenes

A very old esoteric school by now ancient

is the occult school known as Essenes

It is believed one of its followers was Jesus

The Essenes says God is absolute blackness, darkness

God has been seen as light, because humans are frightened of darkness

This is our fear of darkness so we can't conceive of God as blackness

Darkness is eternal, light comes and goes while remaining is darkness

The sun rises and sets into blackness

Yet darkness never rises nor ever sets

Light has some source, Darkness is sourceless

That's why it's infinite and eternal because it's sourceless

# 3 Ways to Immortality

There are three ways to Immortality or Amaroli

The way of the Fakir is the way of physicality

or torture and struggle with the physical body

Fakirs strive to develop physical will, power over the body

they are working on the first room

when the physical will is well developed, then they attain the fourth room

or the possibility of forming the fourth body

but his other functions, rooms, or bodies

like the emotional, intellectual remain undeveloped

she or he has acquired Will but can't use it to gain self-knowledge

The way of the Monk is of religious sacrifice and faith

only a man that has strong religious emotions & imaginations can enter this way

All his work is concentrated on the second body

or room the realm of feelings: All is Godly

subjecting all other emotions to faith's emotion

to develop unity in himself, will over the emotions

in this way motions towards the fourth room

but his physical body and mental capacity remain undeveloped

in order to be able to use what has been attained those two need developing

The way of the yogi is mind and knowledge

the yogi works on the third room by mind development

reaches the fourth room with body and emotions undeveloped

he or she knows everything but can do nothing until these two develop

As on the way of the fakirs or monks,

very few get this understanding of the yogis

that is knowing where it is you're going

# 4th Way to Immortality

For the fourth way you don't have to change the situation

the preparation must be gotten ordinarily and be a very serious one

furthermore there has to be favorable conditions

that is for work on the fourth way, conditions

of life in which at the beginning

of the work, the work finds him

so for him these are natural conditions

The man himself are these conditions

since a man's life normally correspond to it's conditions

The fourth way is named that of the 'sly' one

who knows some secret the others don't own

how this trick was learned is not given and faith isn't needed to be shown

Known is it consists of simultaneously working on the 3 rooms

i.e. while working on the body working on the mind

and emotions all at the same time

while working on the emotions working on the mind

and body or even when working on the mind

working on the body and emotions again at the same time

A whole parallel series of physical, mental, emotional

exercises combine to serve the purpose of becoming immortal

# Dhyana's 4 Stages

Buddhists use the word "dhyana"

For higher states of contemplation

There are four stages in dhyana

First, is one-pointed mind concentration

It excludes desire but not judgement and discernment

Dropping off in stage two is the intellectual function

But the satisfied state of unity remains

In stage three departs that part of satisfaction

Memory returns self-consciousness begins with indifference

At the fourth stage indifference, self-consciousness and memory reach perfection

# 3 Steps of Growth

At first the situation is the master

you are just being dragged by it

You believe that you are, but aren't yet

Secondly, you are, and the situation can't

drag you because you've become a will

In step three you start influencing situations

Just by your being there, it changes

The first phase is of the unenlightened

The second stage is of a constant consciousness

but the seeker has to do something to be conscious

The third state is that of the enlightened

the noteworthy difference is the effortlessness of his consciousness

# Conscious Existence

To become a fully integrated personality means

to complete the circle of existence

From conception individuals pass through birth,

socialization, enculturation, specialization,

an awareness of ego, objectivization of the ego,

realization of the role of culture, perception of creation,

perception of man in cosmic evolution,

the unfolding of unconsciousness and finally

the attainment of a state of conscious existence.

# Echoes & Reflections

The Mystical Rapper, Lover of the Real

Separates the fake: know there's no hate or fear

AMirOR reflects light to see the images clear

REveAL speaks the LA of ever seek his shadow, now hear

The echoes sound let go of E-G-O's set to become one and get free

From the prison of duality, in the world's prism of reality

All light & waves are refracted, fragmented and dispersed throughout totality

Bless the Originator and praise the inventor Edison for electricity

He who brought light here without even saying "let there be"

# Divine Signs

When in us dissolved are all contradictions

Then we are a synthesis of all contradictions

We're talking and yet there is silence

We really love because the need to be loved has left

We are always alone since others can't disturb our aloneness

We are in the crowd but the crowd can never penetrate us

We live in this world but we don't belong to this world

At the center of our being there's no motivation since we've reached the goal

Being choiceless movement and rest rest together

Undivided not renouncing or rejecting we aren't severed

# Clarity of Signals

To be more conscious of the signals we can use a technique named meditation.

By being AWARE of the signals you're receiving (inner, outer)

Meditation is just being a witness, an observer . . .

Remember meditation is the opposite of concentration,

or focusing on one subject, topic, thought, sound . . . etc.

The head-straight, spine-aligned position to be straight is an aim for the chakras or body centers

to connect and for the life force (i.e. the blood, water, oxygen) or energy to move more direct,

fluid, fluent and smooth with less blockage. In effect

the body organs or parts will be in more harmony, tune, unison with each other.

Causing you as a whole to be more receptive to yourself (including your needs, feelings, thoughts, wants)

and becoming CLEAR or perceptive of the signals'

meaning through experience will be leading you to your purpose or reason

of coming into creation as a BEING.

And that helps you function more optimally or live a more fulfilling, complete LIFE.

# Enlightenment is Conscious Sleep

Existence in Ultimate Reality is Oneness

Human problems arise out of human self-consciousness

self-consciousness gives everyone a feeling of being separate

whatsoever we do will go wrong if it is based on separateness

Self-consciousness gives us a feeling that we are the center

and it makes us aware that we're different from others

being self-conscious causes the difference

While we are asleep there is no difference

because we are again merged with the universe

as we lose our self and ego we unite with the universe

Hence so much pleasure comes out of sleep

we feel refreshed, rejuvenated, alive after sleep

all death disappears when we're not separate

who or what's going to die when we're not separate?

For all tantra, yoga, prayer, meditation are to make us aware of inseparateness

and we won't feel insecure or afraid because we are not separate

So enlightenment can also be called conscious sleep

wakefully getting to the same source we move to in deep sleep

# Know Yourself to be Known

When you come to know yourself

then the whole existence will know yourself

Not only will you be looking at existence

looking back at you will be the whole existence

because God is within and without

The Creator is both inside and out

in your self-knowledge you don't feel lonely

until you come to know yourself you feel lonely

Your knowledge isn't a solo thing it's a symphony

not being lonely in your self-knowledge, the whole existence is happy

The whole existence must recognize since we're not strangers to this existence

Being a family, it exists as an interrelated phenomenon does this existence

# Mystical States

Some people's description of a mystic

is a person which believes in thought transference

or someone who believes in the return of spirit

There are 4 qualities that qualify a mystical experience

1 is its ineffability, or incapability to express it

It has to be felt and directly experienced

2nd is the link to things we think, or quality noetic

like Illuminations, Revelations full of significance and importance

Although they remain and prevail they'll be inarticulate

as a law they are a rule for 'after-time' infusing them with a curious sense

3rdly these states are transient, usually two hours seems to be their limit

They're remembered in memory and recognized are their recurrences

recurrences lead to higher consciousness, feeling more important, and innerly rich

Y'all already know mystical states can come from preliminary voluntary operations

mediums like Meditiation, Prayers, Yoga, Sema, Reiki, and Tai Chi

4th the mystic feels as if his own will is in abeyance

and indeed sometimes as if he were held by a superior power though being passive

This peculiarity typically connects mystical states

with certain definite phenomena of alternative personality, such as speeches prophetic

automatic writings or the mediumistic trances

Nonetheless, mystical states are never merely interruptive

some memory of their content always remains as a profound sense of their importance

# 3 Spiritual States

We have 3 spiritual states

In the first we pay no heed to the Most Great

but just keep worshipping and are of service to All

When we get some knowledge of the One in All

then we're aware that we serve nothing other than the One

Again by gaining more consciousness, more silent we become

In that state we don't say "I serve God"

or that "I don't serve God"

We transcend these two degrees

to the extent that 'we don't need to speak'

what is meant is doing from the place of being

for unity to increase we reach the space of witnessing

# 3 types of people

There are three types of people

The first type are the most outward oriented

They collect things that can't be carried to the other shore

Then the second kind collect knowledge, scriptures, theories, philosophies

They're clever but that treasure is a measure of the brain a parcel of the body

And there is the third person whose whole life goal is to be more and more conscious

This consciousness is your innermost self, in the body both worlds exist, this and that

This is of consciousness and that of matter with the interlink being knowledge

Dropping things and knowledge one gets more aware, awake, alert and wise

Here you may appear as a beggar or poor man,

but in the world of consciousness you will be a king

because you will only carry yourself

# 3 Classifications of Humans

Humans can be considered in 3 ways

In terms of the normal,

Abnormal and the Supernormal

Having a happy temperament and mutual love is normal

The abnormal is pathological he has fallen down from the normal

and the supernormal has gone beyond the normal

he or she is healthier and more whole

The supernormal have reached the peak of human's potential

The difference is of negative and positive

The abnormal is negative, whereas, the supernormal is positive

# 3 Basic Personality Traits

They are dependent, controlling, and competitive

Each has its origin in a corresponding stage of personality development

The dependent trait of needing another person

to be complete emanates when you were an infant dependent on parents

The controlling trait of having to be in command

originates from the stage of struggling to master skills of body and language

And the competitive trait of needing to be superior

than others, developed in early school years

when you defined yourself in comparison to other peers

Whichever of these periods predominate is a way to state a person's personality trait

Also under certain circumstances everyone is capable to make

all three responses because everyone is a mix of these traits

# 3 Basic Wisdoms

1.  We always were and are all one

Enacted we'd each cease treating others the way we do

2.  There's enough for all our basic necessities

When shown we'll care to share 'our' things

3.  There's nothing we have to do

Deciding this to be true we'd stop trying to use

"doingness" to solve problems, rather move to

or come from that special space, place of being

That state dissolves problems, seeing

to it the conditions themselves evaporate

which is an important truth for our evolutionary stage

# 3 Points of Knowledge

Knowledge can be divided into three points

The knower, known and knowing

Knowing is a bridge between two points

The subject and the object

Ordinarily knowledge the known reveals

The knower remains unrevealed

Usually our knowledge is one-pointed

It points to the object but not, you, the subject

Unless it starts pointing to, you, the subject

That knowledge will allow you to know the world

But it will not allow you to know yourself

The techniques of meditation are to reveal the knower

So whenever you are knowing something, remember the knower

Don't forget it in the object, also remember the subject

Two ways can be our listening

One the mind can be focused on the speaker but forget the listener

Then you know the speaker but forget the listener

While listening know the speaker and the listener

Then your knowledge is double-pointed, pointing to the known and the knower

Or when you are reading simultaneously be aware of the reader

This is a practice for becoming the third or observer

# Knowledge & Wisdom

Knowledge is heavy, whereas, Wisdom is light

Knowledge is your memory filled with information

Wisdom isn't memory it becomes spread all over your being

Knowledge remains separate it can be forgotten

Knowledge has to be remembered

Wisdom is you it needs no remembering

# Wisdom's Enemies

When a human being begins and learns

we aren't clear about our objectives

In turn, faulty is our purpose, vague are our intentions

We slowly start learning, bit by bit then in gigs

and our thoughts crash when we learn what we never imagined

So we get fearful of the new tasks learning more gives

And so we come across our first natural enemy: fear

It's treacherous, concealed, prowling, waiting for us here

if we run away our quest will be ended

for fear to be hurdled we must be fully afraid and not deny it

just defy it, in spite of it, be alert and the fear disappears

It happens little by little yet suddenly leaves all our fear

Replacing it is clarity of mind allowing us to know and satisfy our desires

clarity of mind is our second enemy because it blinds

it forces us never to doubt, sort of like taking the pleasure route

being brave and courageous since seeing clearly

mistaking this incomplete power that's make believe

it defeats if it leads us to yield and cease growing as a knower

Instead the person may become a clown or buoyant warrior

to overcome that fate we need to defy clarity by using it only for seeing

waiting patiently and carefully measuring the steps we're taking

with this in the witnesses mind that the clarity was almost fooling

and a moment comes when we understand that clarity was just a
point of view

# Wisdom's Enemies continued . . .

Then we'll know in this state that the power is real

our wish becomes the rule we can do whatever we please

Hence, power is the strongest of enemies

the easiest thing to do is give in, being truly invincible

We begin taking risks and end by making rules

being a master we can become cruel

to transcend we need to come to know

the power or force was never yours

just keep going with the flow

and be in line or on course

with conscious progress in evolution's process

continuing onward, forward, toward more knowledge

gradually aging facing the last foe of wisdom's way

old age can't be defeated only fought away

at this stage we have an unyielding desire to rest

if we give in totally, lie down and forget, then we'll regret

being defeated in the last phase of our quest

but when we slough off our tiredness

to live our fate through do we become women and men of wisdom

# The momentary versus the Eternal

The human dilemma: choosing between the momentary and the eternal

If you choose the momentary you're building your house on quicksand, it'll fall

The momentary is just like fuel in the fire of your mind's desire

Only the eternal quenches the thirst of your sole entirely

The eternal can't be chosen since choice is of the momentary

and the next moment will create more hunger, this understood we drop the momentary

You've chosen the eternal the moment the momentary drops

Then you've chosen to build your house on rock-like mountain tops

For that the momentary must become absolutely fruitless

with the momentary failure must be total for it to be meaningless

How can you succeed in this fleeting world of matter?

More important is the home you'll own in life forever and even after!

# The Psychological Regression of Smoking

Whenever we're nervous we've got the tendency to smoke

It keeps us together, it's a psychological regression to smoke

representing being back at our mother's breast

The smoke functions as if we're drinking milk from the breast,

the warmth comes from the hot smoke goin' in,

the smoke almost gives the illusion of milk goin' in,

and the cigarette in the mouth becomes the nipple

like whenever very little children are afraid or angry they'd nibble the nipple

then they would usually relax and calm down

with smoking we're recreating that process now

# The Tree of Life Grounding Exercise

This is a type of meditation practice

which can be done in a group or in solitude

start by sitting or standing straight

begin breathing deeply and rhythmically

As you breathe while your spine is straightening,

Feel the energy, chi, or ki elevate

Imagine your spine is a tree trunk which from its roots

Extend and expand deep into the ground's depth

Enter into the center of earth herself

With each breath from the earth you draw up power

Fathom from the crown of your head

You have branches that sweep up and back down to the earth

Bursting from the crown of your head feel the power

And feel it sweep through the branches till it touches the ground again

Creating a circle making a circuit, like fuses in fusion, returning to the source

Still breathing deeply feel how all our branches intertwine

And the power weaves through them, dances among them

Like the wind blowing the leaves feel it moving inside

Coming to know the feeling of becoming one with the life force

# Cultural Myths vs. Natural Instinct

Cultural Myths inform ethics and behaviors get created from ethics

Problem is our First Cultural Myth varies from our basic instinct

Our First Cultural Myth is that we're inherently evil

aka the myth of original sin says our basic nature is evil

The Second Cultural Myth arises necessarily out of the first

this myth holds that in order to survive we have to be of the fittest

or the survival instinct which has formed much of our societal ethic

Yet our basic instinct is love, oneness, and fairness

it is in our cellular memory and it's our inherent nature

This being our natural instinct it defeats the Myths of Culture

members remember our natural instinct is to reflect the essence of us

Understand the difference between equality and fairness,

our basic instinct is to express uniqueness not sameness

We need systems to allow society to meet the basic survival needs of all individuals

freeing all beings to pursue self-development and creation rather than self-survival

In these societies self-interest and mutual best interest are identical

# Nothing is Pure

In Ultimate Reality

impure or pure is nothing

A saying of tantra that's basic

Hard to believe being without ethics

A message to grow beyond division, really

to transcend dichotomy and duality

Tantra says existence is one

man-made are all distinctions

good-bad, impure-pure, virtue-sin

What's impure or pure depends on your interpretation

So please try and don't divide

lest you want to be divided

# Salt-Water Purification Technique

Salt and water are both cleansing elements

Water washes and salt preserves, serves as a disinfectant

The ocean, or womb of life, is salt water

so are tears helping us to purify the heart of all that bothers

This is a meditation which helps when

we are anxious, stressed, or depressed

Fill your ritual chalice or any cup up

with water add three mounds of salt

stir it with the cup in your lap

let hatred, fears, worries, doubts, disappointments attract

in your mind see them as a muddy stream

that flows out of you as you breathe

and by the salt water is dissolved

allow enough time to feel deeply cleaned, now uphold the cup

Breathe deeply and feel yourself drawing up power from the earth

let the power flow into the salt water until you can see it glowing lighter

sip the water, and as you feel it on your tongue

know now you've taken in the power of the one

You've taken in the changing power of cleansing, healing

that transformed your former fear and unhappiness

Finally, empty the leftover water into a flowing stream

usually the nearest is running down the kitchen sink

# Simplicity

To live without ideals is simplicity

for ideals create division hence complexity

Interest in being somebody else causes complexity

and being content with yourself as you are is simplicity

Simplicity means to be just yourself, true, real

in tremendous acceptance of whosoever you are with no ideal

Ideals bring the split and cause conflict

The bigger the ideal, the bigger the split

With yourself being in harmony

is simplicity's significant beauty

# Our Mind is like a Mirror

Like a mirror is the original mind

It remains pure and retains its purity

But dust can gather on rather cover up the purity

This is the condition of the ordinary mind

If it was possible for any impurity

Then there would be no way to regain purity

Once you know how to clean, clear the dust from the mind

You've reached all that's necessary for growing

You've received all that's worth knowing

In the East, we're believed to be divine

Whereas, in the West we're believed to have sinned

Somewhere at some point in time, since

In the West they falsely identify their being as the mind

The dust is all your past what you've known and experienced

To regain the original mind means being free from those experiences

So with the past and all that is dust just don't identify

Whatsoever you know is always of the past, and you're in the present

You know meditation's a method to remove yourself from the past and be in the present

This is a technique to attain the state of the original mind

# Religious & Political Minds

A political mind always wants to change the world

because it thinks the problem is the world

A religious mind thinks I am wrong, that's why the world is wrong

It is through me the world becomes right or wrong

and says unless I change myself there can be no change

The politician says the world has to be changed

since the world isn't the problem they only create more problems

Religious people change themselves for that is only possible

and through that transformation, the world is transformed

because we are each vital parts of the whole

The transformation is possible when we come to realize our no-bodiness

it's possible only when we come to realize our no-thingness

# Rebels & Revolutionaries

The ecstatic people or angels are the rebels

They want to live as individual soles

and don't like any rigid social structure in the world

also they don't want to replace societies

Revolutionaries want to change societies

revolutionaries desire some other man-made structures,

rebels don't trust those forced structures

they're anarchic, not wanting to rule or be ruled

trusting nature if left alone everything will be beautiful,

but we have become so neurotic that we can't live without rulers

# Morality & Religion

Morality exists on respectability and methods of refining the ego

But Religion is a spiritual transformation through the dissolution of the ego

Morality says leave that which is wrong

Religion says leave that which is false

In Spirituality that which is true has value

And for Morality what is right is given value

So morality depends on the ego known to be a false entity

Whereas, Spirituality transcends the ego to get to reality

# Religion & Science

The Western mind has been searching

for the theoretical component of existence

the causal link for how things are happening

what is the cause and how to control the effects

The Eastern mind has been searching

to find the aesthetic component of reality

not how to manipulate nature or to be conquering

but in how to be in a deep friendship or participation with it, really

Religion is a love relationship like the Eastern mind

The Western mind is scientific, a struggle and fight

Science is aggressive, Religion is receptive

So religion is feminine and science is masculine

# Business Crisis

A businessman is one who's busy

buying, selling, investing interest in things

Things which bring in money

For them if it doesn't make money

then it's not worthwhile and doesn't make sense

They can lose their sole in search of fool's gold, it goes to that extent

for the value of faith and virtue of natural laws can't be converted into saleable objects

Their top priority being money, at times morals, principles and even rules are broken

A businessman's whole concern is about things not about persons

usually this type of person is continuously busy never at rest

since there is more to be put into banks, stocks, wallets and purses

Also their health is an issue because risks cause anxiety, worry, or nervousness

Only the businessman dies for they accumulate things

and death takes away those accumulated things

# Political Power Move

Usually politicians are the most jealous people

because their life depends on being successful, famous, powerful

Their whole longing is to be more and more powerful

Most politicians can't be friends of each other

because they're competing for their goal making them against each other

Politicians talk of peace, while their nations aren't at peace with each other

unless politics loses importance, war will be part of its game

The way out of the political trap is to make

people more and more free-economically, politically, spiritually

decentralize power, the government that governs the least is the most beneficial

but the whole trend is going in the opposite direction

Countries are hiding their lust for power greed in the name of nationalization

nationalizing industries and so on, so more power goes to the state

It becomes the only owner and then the whole economy is controlled by the state

then there is no freedom left to and for the people

and the politician, as the state gains power, becomes more and more powerful

The only way to take away the power of politicians being

to de-nationalize things and in-corporate beings

# Politicians are Bad Magicians

Our fellow leaders or chosen speakers are bad magicians

we're forced to follow the path and decisions of politicians

suffering from their narrow one-track minded visions of division

never surrendering, preferring to bravely fight the pharaoh within

I'm Light & Wave surfing on Cupid's arrow uniting the heart's wisdom

Conversing to say delight and save the light for our peace and freedom

# As many worlds as minds

This always remains a basic question:

How to change something

For example how to change negatives into positives

Don't try, you can't. But if you're positive then nothing is negative

All that exists around you, you're its source

Know you are the creator of your world

And remember we're not living in One world

As many minds there are, there are worlds

Each mind is living, giving birth to its own world

You're a reflection in the mirror that is the world

# One World

Let's be for the West fulfilling needs of the East

And the East fulfilling needs of the West

We need to settle with mettle for our best interest

Not being disagreeing, different, or divided

This whole world has to become one to survive

There needs to be only one single humanity

Then there will be an enormous release of energies

The East has treasures in religious technologies

The West has treasures in scientific technologies

And if both can meet this world will become Paradise

I am all for one world, one humanity, and ultimately one science

That will take care of religion and science, both

The science which will take care of the inner and outer both

# Religion Is Non-Social

When we experiment with witnessing

also known as observation, or meditation

all that's repressed will have to be witnessed

whatever is buried will have to be faced

we have to create eyes where we've become blind

we need to awaken in us all that is asleep

and will have to return to the point we lost energy as a child

learning that state is undivided, uninterrupted pure energy

Knowing all religiousness is just a reclaiming of our childhood

or a way of getting free from the injustices of society

this is why religion can never be social, has to be understood

that's the reason society never accepts a religious person

because rebellion is the basic stance of the religious person

and their essential process is to demolish injustices of society

take away wherever they've paralyzed, blocked, or stolen energy

real religious people aim to make us whole and free us completely

So society is essentially anti-religion and religion is essentially anti-society

# Mysticism

Mysticism is the varying sole of religion

It comes from these two words "myein & mysterion"

Mysterion in Greek means some secret ceremony

And myein means to keep one's mouth closed about the ceremony

Mysticism is the experience that life's not logic but poetry

It's the declaration that life can never be known essentially

Mysticism consists of three categories the known, unknown, and unknowable

and that is the essential core of it all

Experienced but not known can be the unknowable

it can't be reduced to a form of knowledge

Being basically schizophrenic for it requires division does knowledge

knowledge says that the object has to be separated from the subject

In mysticism the seeker becomes one with the sought

the lover dissolves into the beloved

in such unity knowledge is impossible

in such unity there is only experience

this which is within you that's experiencing

Mysticism means you've seen, experienced

something that can't be expressed

Those who've touched the unknowable gather together to share

you should know it cannot be a verbal kind of sharing

their sharing is of their spiritual being

into each other they pour their being

# Kabbalah

Kabbalah means "receiving" or "that which has been received"

It's the Jewish mystical tradition from ancient wisdom

That has many layers of meaning, symbolism and allusions

Also its main contents contains ten sefirots

Which came from the Endless or Ein Sof

The 1st sefirah describes Ein Sof by negations, called Ayin or Nothingness

In this primal state God is undifferentiated being, or no-thingness out of the depth of Nothingness,

Shines the primordial point of Hokhmah, Wisdom the 2nd sefirah

This point expands into a circle of Understanding the 3rd sefirah Binah

Binah is the womb, the Divine Mother which receives the seed of Hokhmah

She gives birth first to Hesed (Love) and (Power) Gevurah

Gevurah and Hesed, respectively, are the left and right arms of God

Two poles of the Divine personality: judgement, grace and free-flowing Love

For the world to function properly both are necessary and needed

Ideally a balance is achieved symbolized by the central sefirah Tif'eret

Or (Beauty) also called Rahamim (Compassion), for if judgement

Is not softened by Love, it then lashes out and threatens

To destroy life, here lies the origin of evil called Sitra Ahra the Other Side

Evil originates in divine thought, that eliminates waste before emanating life

Tif'eret is the trunk, he is called Heaven, Sun, King, and Holy One

Blessed be he, the standard Rabbinic name for God, He is the Son

Of Hokhmah and Binah the next two sefirot are Netsah and Hod

Netsah is Eternity the right leg, left leg is Splendor or Hod

These are also the source of prophecy, the foundation Yesod

Is the 9th sefirah and represents the phallus also called Tsaddiq, the righteous 1

The righteous 1 is the foundation of the world or axis mundi,

The cosmic pillar its light and power are channeled to the last sefirah, Malkhut

Malkhut (Kingdom) is also known as Shekhinah or Presence

# A Sufi

Sufis don't separate themselves by opinion or dogma

for they realize the heart as the Shrine of God

So Sufism is the heart's sect, cult, or religion

and Sufis desire to remove the false self and discover God within

Sufis teach Love, Peace, and being Happy

Sufis seek Illumination and see Harmony

They give Love to all created things

and they get a greater Power of Love from the Creator of Beings

# Ecstasy

Ecstasy is a language that we have forgotten

we have been forced or compelled to forget it

civilizations and societies are against it

since the society has a huge investment

in misery, it feeds, it survives on misery it depends

Society is no longer for human beings

It is using humans for its self-means

Society has become more important than humanity

the culture, the civilization, the church have become a higher priority

now they are not for humans as they were meant to be

Every child is born in ecstasy

very natural for kids is ecstasy

it is part of being alive, life is ecstasy

children bring it into the world, then comes society

with its living conditions creating this apparent misery

Society is neurotic it hasn't allowed people to be in ecstasy

for those ecstatic pose dangers and are threatening

Understanding the mechanism things get to be easy

they can't control a person in ecstasy

it's impossible, they can only control people in misery

An ecstatic woman/man is bound to be free

because freedom is an element of ecstasy

# Elements of Ecstasy

Because LAshaun had long-lasting sex with me

i came to know these 3 Elements of Ecstasy

Foremost, I transcended time completely

lost track of the past, her presence future surpassing

landing lovely here in the moment-present fully

feeling thoughtless one with existence wholely

Knowing no me where souls meet, we

were and the 'I' was absent egolessness is the 2$^{nd}$ quality

or element and 3$^{rd}$ of all gone was culture, civilization, society

I was natural like the cows, birds, and trees

leaving the masked faces of facades behind kindly

taken in by the current of the cosmos floating flowingly

from the infinite source for what seemed an eternity

These transcendences happen through existential experience not ideology

Therefore, ignorance can only lead you to hypocrisy

# Choicelessness is Euphoric

The more we move in opposites

The quicker becomes evolution's process

And the deeper, wider, higher it's progress

Of not much help will be just happiness

Or only struggle, because there'll be no challenges

Both are necessary, life exists between opposites

As a subtle tension in which you won't choose

And there'll be no struggle when this is understood

You'll move in tune with life's grooves and moods

Keep goin' on growin' and knowin' both are good

Feelings, thoughts showin' that to be naturally true

Being a witness you'll be euphoric when you don't choose

# 3 Kinds of Freedom

First there is a freedom you're already acquainted with

this is a FREEDOM FROM

For example, a worker wants to be free from the boss

It's a reaction of the ego asserting itself

Since it's a reaction rather than something you fathom

or deeply understand you're bound to change jobs

but that's not real freedom

Second kind of freedom is FREEDOM FOR

We want to be free for doing our own thing

This is our self-will in action

Third type of freedom is neither for nor from

It's not a reaction or an action

solely a state named Being

Some holy sages call it seeing

# Getting out of Emotional Debt

Feelings need to be expressed

to not be stored in emotional debt

There are three sorts of emotional debt

the first is reactive emotional debt

or a momentary delay between injury and hurt's expression

Recent emotional debt is a longer delay that hurts are stored as resentment

Remote emotional debt includes unresolved hurt from the past

these remote feelings get activated by recent pain that reminds you of the past

the preoccupation with an immediate emotion before it's expressed

is known as reactive emotional debt

the discomfort of holding in the feeling, has gotten you

to want to let it out as soon as possible

which if pushed away your feeling get stored in recent emotional debt

if you keep delaying expressing feelings it'll result in remote emotional debt

your feelings build to explosive levels and at times break free of defenses

and are often expressed out of control and out of context

so others can't understand or sympathize with your exaggerated expressions

leading to further alienation, loneliness and a sense of helplessness

and then whenever you attempt to make emotional contact, others get hurt

the process feeds on itself producing more anger, anxiety, guilt and hurt

# Inner Richness is Lasting

Those who have wasted lives gaining worldly things

can't enter the Kingdom of God, ones who attain the inner are welcomed in

ones who have possessed much but not themselves are poor

If you possess yourself you're truly rich and can never ever be poor

Since others eyes reflect your achievements in the world

know no eye can reflect your real inner sole

When others think you're poor they judge by your clothes

now some accumulate things to not be seen as poor folks

Remember your identity consists of your outer reflection

members can only reflect things they can't reflect your essence

# From Beggar to Emperor

Of existence thought can give you only a minimum

whereas, feeling can give you the maximum

through the mind there is no way to existence

through the heart is the only way I am existing

So feel it through the heart for existence to be yours

feel it, be grounded in it, and know this overflowing to be yours

you, who, possess totality, the deepest possibility

The centermost core of existence is your reality

you'll come to know that this mysterious universe belongs to you

and more so that this existence has been existing for you

By being rooted you become one with the whole entirety

knowing the existence exists for you, you become an emperor suddenly

# Masks

One who applies a set of attitudes almost all the time

is the mark of the confirmed skeptic

who remains doubtful about all topics about the spirit

from the presence of God to the possibility of an afterlife

They move very slowly on the way of light

and deny they have any fear of emptiness and abandonment

but they have more than others their mask is just so deceptive

Highly successful people who owe their achievements

to struggle and competitiveness tend to wear the mask of self-confidence

to not look at hidden beliefs maybe in God's defiance

they act on personal power and self-will rejecting surrenderance

The mark of someone who moves very fast on the path

paradoxically, the more turbulent you are inside the quicker you're moving

A prerequisite for waking up is in complete disillusionment

because the whole notion that you're a fixed entity is a great illusion

and the sooner you see you're complex the sooner you'll drop the mask of egoism

# Our Various Bodies

The outermost layer of all is the flesh or physical body

This is visible, experiences pain and death: the physical body

The next body is known as the aura or astral body

It's lighter and finer than the quality of the physical body

its need is to encase the soul on the astral plane

like the physical body is necessary on the earthly plane

The time the physical body dies and the soul leaves the earthly plane

The soul withdraws into the astral body somewhere in the astral plane

Inside the astral body but quite different from it is the causal body

It's much finer in quality than the astral as the astral is of the physical body

It is the sheath wherein we find the planted cause of our karma aka the seed body

The next sheath around soul is that which we know as the mental body

or seed mind for this corresponds to the implanted karma of the causal body

# Our 4 Bodies

The 1$^{st}$ is the Physical or Carnal body

this is also called the "Carriage" body

The 2$^{nd}$ body is the Natural body

or "Horse" which deals with desires, feelings aka the Astral body

The 3$^{rd}$ is the Spiritual body

this is the "Driver" and mind, the Mental body

The 4$^{th}$ body is the Divine body

"Master" also the I, consciousness, will called the Causal body

The functions of the physical body

correlate to the functions of other bodies

It's automaton working by external influences,

the natural bodies' desires are produced by automaton,

the spiritual bodies' thoughts proceed from desires,

the divine bodies' different and contradictory will is formed from desires

The body obeys desires and emotions subject to intelligence,

emotional powers and desires obey thought and intelligence,

thinking functions obey consciousness and will

Then come the I the Consciousness and the Will

# Our 3 Centers

Head, Heart and Navel

The head and heart are peripheral centers

The original center is the navel

also called the hara, or our real center

this is the center of being

The heart's center is in feeling

The center of the head is in knowing

Knowing is the farthest from being

nearer is the center of feeling

which is needed to bridge reason to being

Religion is concerned with being

Poetry is concerned with feeling

and Philosophy is concerned with knowing

# The 2 Feelings

Being happy is liking the way you feel

not being happy is not liking the way you feel

There are only two feelings: pleasure and pain

The way you experience pain

and the name you give it depend on when occurs the pain

Pain in the present is experienced as hurt

Hurt is experienced as sadness the realization of loss or disappointment

Pain in the future is perceived as anxiety

Pain in the past is remembered as anger

Unexpressed anger, redirected and held within is guilt

It requires energy to redirect anger

This depletion of energy is called depression

# Doubt and Trust

Science is based on doubt

It's method is to doubt

Science can't exist without doubt

The object is not to be trusted

Religions method is of trust

Concerning itself with subjectivity is its must

Just religions journey is inwards

And sciences journey is outwards

They're diametrically opposite but also complementary

Obviously, as opposites always are complementary

Between opposites there is a synchronization

The inner and the outer are in coordination

It is like inhalation and exhalation

Which are two aspects of the same phenomenon

When we're able to bring the harmonization

Between doubt and trust then we'll reach completion

For through doubt we can get to know the object

And with trust we can get to know the subject

# Trust in Doubt

Whenever we do believe

then and there enters disbelief

Disbelief is a shadow of belief

belief naturally brings disbelief

First is belief, secondary is disbelief

Stopping beliefs drops disbelief

Starting to trust in our doubt

we'll adjust within and figure out

that what was inside real doubt

transforms within and turns around

into true trust just being found

Trust and doubt are within, belief is from out

# ALoneness & Loneliness

These are two totally different states of being

When you miss the other, you're lonely

And when you enjoy yourself, it's aloneness

When you're happy, full, light you're alone

When you're empty, blank, dark you're lonely

Loneliness is misery, it's a suffering hollowness

Aloneness is ecstasy, it's enjoying all-oneness

# Sin and Virtue

Sin and Virtue are coins of society

Virtue is as much of a wealth as is money

like money virtue is also a social recognition

and so is sin, too, a social recognition

Virtue and Sin are societies' currencies

We first accumulate wealth and currency

then we create a bank balance of being virtuous

hoping this bank balance of virtue will go with us

# Battle Rap Tappin' Mics

Don't think, blink and I'll blow by like A.I.

Know this fly guy's sided with the Most High

That's why the show-stopper goes coast to coast more than a globe-trotter

Flow hotter, lines shine brighter light at the end, the champ is unsigned

Designed and destined to be the dream of the top, cream of the crop

Dropping unrehearsed verses is my bread and butter

The Soul of Hip-Hop got this game zip-locked

Air tight to put your fire out, no desire is the higher route

I'm the one they talk about, moshed on crowds

climbed the bean stalk now I walk on clouds

Angelic will taught me to be the jack of all trades

Flash Gordon to John Blaze striking James' Flames

Don't wanna not gonna stop being up to date

Raps are my craze just what my mind state craves

I'm rhyme inclined I've trained/taught thoughts of my brain

To be entwined with rhythmic sound waves in O so many light rays

# The Origin of Hip-Hop & Rap

Yo I want all of you out there to know

that rap's roots are deeper than 30 years old

Around 3,000 years ago there was a fellow

by the name of David who was a prophet of his time

he would deliver divine messages in the form of rhyme

or rap, if, that's defined as modern day poetry

so there were many who came and left poetry

About 800 years ago, born was Rumi

now known as the most mystical of rappers

with him also came a spiritual ritual dance

a trance-like whirling meditation called Sema

in which participants would spin counter-clockwise

the moment they had the feeling or vibe

It is said it has to come unforced, otherwise

it couldn't be accepted by the Most High

Now fast forward to the 21$^{st}$ century, while

we have a growing hip-hop culture worldwide

With DJ's playing records, mixing, cutting, scratching

B-boys and girls spinning on their heads break dancing

graffiti artists like cavemen carving, tagging on walls paint spraying

I'm just writing these words from my sole for the one

to let you know where we've originally come from

# Tip-Top Si

O so High and deeply kneeling in the World Wide Web

I already feel like a really old soul, how about a retired vet

God that's odd cause I haven't even begun my career yet

Unsigned so for my songs never got a paycheck

Or ever performed on any platform or stage-set

I just blessed the mic with raps on tracks all seventy 7, yes

Wishing each much success in life's every facet/ aspect

Hoping we treat other brothers, sisters with more respect

RIP to 2 P A C, O D B, B I G, Pun, Cobain, Marley, Pavarotti, Vivaldi: God Bless

All players, singers, rockers, rappers past & present

I'm here to praise the classes' essence

2 See A Sea, I say cheers so raise your glasses and let

The liquid lesson's fluidly and fluently begin

Liquor before beer, now know no fear to drink again!

# Do say what's meant to pay the rent

To Fifee—Heehee wi wi si si Miss E see me PeePee with my itsi bitsy ini mini mi ni ti ni tiny TeePee be me in an NY beanie baby lady im crazy mad insane in love with ALL the above when push comes to shove with care bear hug the hand to land and stand under a snug glove over sands hover on a rugged rug~

thank u 4 that child's vu> im a fan of all that's wet wild pure real and true HU . . . Man is this shit hitting the fan or what Mam? PU!!! The farting shitheads stink, the sinking ships wrecked if they aren't overbored I'm hitting the deck; swimming to get to the whole and holy shore and for reminding those who forgot or doubt to trust letting go of fear is a must for love to be more pure of that you can be sure and rest assured.

Is it right Am I a meanie I am not meaning to be de-meaning it's d'evil demons demonstrating cruel intentions intent not meant to mention in an indented sentence; sent to u your presence a present in the present tense: intensely invest in sense the interest is the Essence

AlexiA words can not say how much I wanted to C B with U when/while I was there in Paris, France and I can't explain why I didn't feel like coming-At the time I know I was working from home for home (home being the space/place/body/heart) + (time=the mind)

Combine hear here to see a sea there (sea=spirit,soul,the sole,the whole,the all-one) HU We came from and for, to get her (together) and come home.

# Land of the Brave & Home of the Free

Fe fi fo fum Se si so sum Be bi bo bum He hi ho hum um mum . . .

oh hi ho (Ohio) Miss our I I da ho Am Erica whore I abhor where's virgin Virginia's

Mary land I adore a door in da corridor in d core a door in décor a door in d echo's a door

-oh hi ho I da ho from Mary land and unscramble uncle sam to understand

peeping toms elves eaves dropping eves often on ten of ten coffins coughin (limbs)

fins of finnigan again in (limbo) Missis sippi with the dixie chicks kicking it wit sixty-six sexy seek hips and hippies lips dicklicking pixie stix in pippies long stocking shocking king

ritchie rich itch tickling to tickle nipples and irk dirk digglers worm for work of digging dirt

the big flirt who lifts skirts'n'shirts off turned on, horny and anxious persons . . .

Miss E I miss U hippie pippie hit me silly till im a bit feely wit a really tipsy gipsy quick a quickie quickALI. Wile E'll free willy willing, while shes willingly wit me it be I LA RIMA

Si as Si co-signA

Ya ALLa Obama Hussein i might be coming to your casa blanca as early as late December

If D C and the ones Washing the Tons are wanting and wishing me to get there

im so Excited no I can't hide it I confide in U there's a word to look ^ up

to find the meaning and purpose it serves i don't mean to disturb you

or get on your nerves no sir E sorry for his story [history]

it is up ^ to us just US to bring JUSTice

into this corrupt mix-up of risky business + tricky politics

busy mess of many tics

# Local, Global & Total Warning

This gift of gab with precision is to get the facts: there are only presences no persons

In existence the sole is the only thing that exists and the rest are myths

Never missed for forever persists and consists of this instance

So know the 1 is the source for the force to be with you O B 1

Can O B Jedi, but really seriously O can only B 1

I rap and keep flowing to show the Essence of Life

Come and go back to grow from the past experiences and get the lessons of Life

So let's show the audience more the exact presents of Life, is the presence of Light

& the gift is Sound which is all around echoes never die always alive are reflections of light

Detections of Life on other planets have yet to be found but there is enough evidence revealed

Tests have shown relevant elements and vital signs abound that conditions are possible for ET's

Now let's touch down the solid ground that which can be felt, life's facts ice caps eventually melt

As well oil reserves will gradually deplete, there is a hole in the Ozone, O LORD how can we help

Not take for granted and protect home the planet you planted in the universe, Earth is our world

Will you let a select few get to know you and your plan for the net to be rescued from the 3<sup>rd</sup> War

# Law of CivilizAtion

Collins Concise Dictionary defines "civilization":

as a society that has a complex cultural, political & legal organization

Laws are needed to keep societies in order and operation

to control tendencies of crime, conflicts and destruction

social order must be justly enforced with consistency

Also man-made laws can change if flaws cause inhumanity

and that may mean separating governments from religion, if necessary

for the improvement in lives of beings nationally and internationally

# Defenses

Yo, you know if you had no defenses

you wouldn't have any emotional debts

you'd be free, freely showing your feelings

regardless of them being painful or pleasing

others would give you your room

cease or continue to love you

If they chose not to love you

because of what you spoke it'd be their problem

you wouldn't regret what you couldn't prevent

rather your life will be filled with a sense of self confidence & respect

You'd experience pain in a visceral way, w/o the intervention of your defenses

without feeling bad your hurt and anger you'd express

you'd react to anxiety as a signal to get ready to defend yourself

but you wouldn't feel any shame

you, like all others, would make mistakes

accept responsibility for whatever damage you caused

then you'd know you can manage to grow by working on your flaws

# The Ego

A by-product of the natural course of life is the ego

No being can evolve without being involved with the ego

The ego is just like the shell of the egg, so

It's needed to protect, like the shell of the seed, yo

But the protection can become dangerous also

When it goes on protecting and doesn't allow the seed to grow

Everyone is born as a seed, the outer cover being the ego

It needs to go the time it hinders the inner being to grow

Initially ego is needed, eventually necessary is transcending the ego

If someone dies as a seed, she or he has died with the ego

Died without really attaining the destiny that was possible

Without actually attaining the conscious existence that was possible

# Silence

When you have become silent, then

to what others are saying you will not pay attention

if opinions are important like you need others to certify it

or somehow approve of it, you are not silent

but the moment you're really quiet, still, silent

Now you're not disturbed by the outside

and don't become affected inside

for here you're whole

or one with your sole

# Surrender

Being completely, totally open is love that's pure

It's dangerous, we're vulnerable and may become insecure

We can't ask how to love or how to surrender

but we can know how we're preventing surrendering

If we haven't yet fallen in love

we have to find out why we haven't loved

The reason being our defense structure of the ego

this false "I" which isn't is the ego

The moment you come to feel "I am not", then

that is the moment surrender happens

# Soundless Sound

Mantras are meaningless sounds

of necessity they're pure sounds

The soundless sound you can hear

when you plug or close your ears

The absence of sound is a very subtle experience

it creates the opportunity to fall back upon ourselves

With sounds we move away and unto the other

with sounds we relate or communicate to the other

and through soundlessness we return to ourselves

that's why techniques use soundlessness to move within ourselves

# Technique of No-Technique

Two thousand years ago Bodhidharma

introduced Zen Buddhism to China

He was an Indian monk who believed in no-technique

For Ch'an or Zen is based on no-technique

Zen masters say if "you" do something you'll miss

because of the division between doer and doingness

Zen says the mind has to drop into the heart

then that paves the way for us to learn life's art

of being now here receiving gifts of the present

Notice with the mind we're either ahead or behind in the past

Know this that the mind tries to use supports

like praying places or holy books are supports

and Zen says the truth can't be borrowed

so no tradition or master is needed to be known

for us to attain truth and become actualized

we must gain it alone for ultimate freedom to be realized

# Tantra

Tantra says move wholely in sex completely

Forget yourself, civilization, religion, culture, ideology

Forget everything just move in the sex act totally

Don't leave anything out become absolutely non-thinking

Only then does the awareness happen that you've become one with someone

Then it can be detached from the partner and this feeling of oneness

Can be used with the whole of creation

Once you know how to create this circle

It can be made without and within, since this cycle

Comes from being created of woman and man

because you were created by these two you are both woman and man

When the circle is made within your inner woman is meeting your inner man

And only when this circle is created is real celibacy attained

When this circle is created inside freedom you've gained

Tantra says sex is the deepest bondage

yet it can be used for the highest freedom

Tantra even says poison can be used as medicine, albeit with wisdom

So don't condemn anything rather use it

Find out ways how it can be used as a solution

Tantra is a deep total acceptance of life

It is the only approach of it's kind

All the religions are afraid of sex

Because such a great energy is sex

Once you are in it no more, then

The current will take you anywhere, hence fear begins

But don't make a barrier in which you and the current become two

Do allow this vital energy to have power over you

For Tantra says this current is you

# Kundalini

Tantra says the range of mental experience can be expanded

helped by the senses your mind can have experiences

within the framework of object, time and space

But there can also be a mind frame

that transcends the state of object, time, or space

which can happen when the present mind breaks

the familiar chain of limits and definitions

going past the borders, energy is released from these experiences

These experiences have been named nirvana, moksha, emancipation,

self-realization, salvation, samadhi or liberation

Contrary to popular belief these states never cease, levels end to begin again

From the start of creation yogis and tantrics have become

aware that in this physical body there is a potential force

that's not psychological, philosophical, or transcendental but a dynamic potential force

in the material body and it's called kundalini

The greatest discovery of yoga and tantra is this kundalini

# Life is sex energy

Tantra says sex energy is life energy

The word sex isn't confined to the act or reproduction

for the whole play of sex is with life energy

Wherever negatives and positives meet, sex is the function

Tantra Masters say listening is passive and feminine

and that speaking is active and masculine

The speaker is the one who's penetrating

while the listener is the one who's receiving

so between the two a sex act is happening

For the message to enter and become illuminating

the listener has to be totally passive

not thinking for that will make her active

Tantra says that when our - and + poles unite

it means the union of our masculine and feminine sides

Members remember we are both woman and man

because we are the effects of the cause of woman and man

# Sex Is Spiritual

For spiritual sex our whole body must be relaxed

then the sex experience spreads all over the body

our every cell is bathed in it and there's a peak, we'll know that

when we've known sex that there's a peak in which we're not a body

In deep sex we aren't a body just a hovering spirit,

our bodies will be left behind or forgotten completely

and there comes a feeling of being fulfilled

a feeling that there is no need to desire anything

Only humans achieve this spirituality in sex, otherwise it's just animal instinct

If this is difficult to believe you haven't experienced it or else you'll be understanding

# 2 types of OrgasM

One type of orgasm is coming to the peak of excitement

we can call this a peak orgasm

and there is another named valley orgasm

In the beginning necessary for both is excitement

For the first excitement has to be intense

you have to help it grow toward the peak

To get the valley orgasm we use another technique

Excitement is only a beginning in the second

Once the man has entered both can relax

only if the erection is in shrinkage then a little movement

as to resurrect the erection just that much excitement

but then again the man and woman relax

this deep embrace can be held for hours with no ejaculation

On the contrary in ordinary sexual action

or peak we meet as excited beings seeking climax

and reaching orgasm we get depleted of our energy

but in the tantric orgasm we gain and regain energy

# Third Eye

If our two eyes become static, like stones, nonmoving

through them the energy will stop flowing

They only move because of the flow of energy

the vibration and movement is the cause of energy

Staring at a spot without allowing the eyes to move elsewhere gives a staticness

suddenly the energy will not be moving through these two lens

Eyes can be static but energy cannot be static

if the eyes are closed to the energy, the energy tries to find a new path, which

the nearest is the third eye just between the eyebrows, deep half an inch

like water flows and you close one hole it'll find another to tap in

and the closest one with the least resistance, that is

it will find it automatically

we don't have to do anything specifically

other than stop the energy moving through the physical eyes

for the energy to move through the spiritual eye

This opens doors to new views of perception

It also makes way for more dimensions of sensations

# Identities Bridge

If you love a woman or man,

just sit by their side and feel identified

as if you are the beloved

and let the other feel they're you, the lover

Wait and feel identified, suddenly you'll be surprised

by both having a shock of energy

Both will feel that some energy

has moved from each other to the other

Lovers have felt energy jump like electric shocks do to reach the other

Whenever you are identified with something there's a bridge

and the energy can move through that bridge

# We're Together

We're together forever, I swear

We were never ever severed, you heard

BAHRAM's verse first; PishRo's second, if ya had a thirst

For English I'll quench it in this the third

Lyrics surged to merge, submerged

Solely united for certain, certainly earth concerned

Only time I got the urge to curse in my conversation is to convert Satan

Cause that's the only playa hatin'

Wanna, gonna change the station, down with Osama

Safer saner haven is what we cravin', so up with Obama

Much local love, national congratulations, and global celebration

Day after marches, festivals, parades and ovations

Another chapter starts, high hopes and great expectations

But not to be unsaid, one brother can only do so much

War-torn, heart-broken lover's don't get your hopes up

Living life's an art, practice it in peace, for each one to teach one

The impotence of feeling lonely and divided

And the importance of being uniquely united

# Wow, Now Vows of Marriage

I am marrying not for reasons of security

Knowing the only real security

Isn't in owning or possessing

Not for demanding or expecting

And not even in hoping, wishing

My life's needs, the other, will be fulfilling

I know everything I need in life

All the love, understanding and insight

That compassion, passion and wisdom reside within

So I am marrying you in hopes of giving these gifts

Not for controlling, limiting, or hindering you

From the honest celebration and expression that's true

Which is the highest and best within you, deep inside

Wishing that for all aspects of your being and facets of your life

I see marriage as producing opportunities

Rather than as producing obligations

Opportunities for lifting our lives to their optimum potential

For the ultimate reunion with God through the communion of our souls

# It's so Major to Savor the Flavors

We know we can't live without eating

but we eat them very unconsciously, robotlike, automatically

If the taste isn't lived, you're just stuffing

Go slow be aware of what it is you're tasting

don't go on just swallowing things

Taste them with no hurry or rush to become what you're tasting

and then it can be felt all over the body

not just in the mouth or on the tongue but all over the body

Allow the ripples to spread and fill the whole of your body

Be more sensitive and alive to feel more of your body

also for more life to enter your inner being

then your food intake quantity will decrease and its quality will increase

# Delight & Joy

When you're delighted you'll feel joy descending on you

Then joy is divine and delight is human

Hence it's important to sing, celebrate, and dance

Delight creates the capacity to receive the joy that's not in our hands

The response of delight creates the heart, opens its chambers' doors

We can delight in small things, but joy is of the whole

Delight can be expressed and for joy expression is impossible

# Happiness comes from being needed

The more mechanical devices do things

The less we become relevant or needed

The more we feel useless, futile, meaningless

The computer is slowly replacing beings

Happiness comes out of being needed

Because then you feel your being has meaning

And that without you there will be a difference

The modern mind continuously feels a meaninglessness

Due to the feeling of not being needed

When we feel in the world we are needed

Then we have a significance and meaning

Technology has made better homes, not better women and men

Because for better women and men needed is some other dimension

That dimension is of awareness not of mechanicalness

# Deep Need

We have a deep need to be needed

Somebody must need us otherwise we'll feel

That we don't have any ground under our feet

For the great majority, society is their need

Like lovers say: "I love you" but they want to be loved

As if they love in order just to be loved

Only one whose need to be needed has disappeared can love

When we're egoless with a sole that's crystallized happens real love

Jesus has somewhere said: "Blessed are the solitary and elect,

For they shall find the kingdom they came from and will go there again."

# True Value

The great majority seek refuge and shelter in money

The language of the majority of people is money

Most of us measure people mainly by their money

As if the amount we have is the weight of our soul

As if when we've got no money, we've got no soul

But wealth in whatever currency is only external

And you and your soul were and are always internal

Their dimensions are different they're 2 different worlds

So don't measure another by what they have in the world

It's more precise to perceive others by what they do to the world

# Response of E-Mails

Hi HIGH ALi,

I hope all is well with you, your brother Human, your mom + the whole family

I miss you guys so much ☺ words cannot say enough about true Love.

Truly, you are in my heart and on my mind at all times in all spaces.

In fact, it really did not take long for me to adapt to my natural habitat.

As you know I am in the presence of family-

so I'm in a warm climated environment with four seasons,

more reasons to feel securely at home being embraced in mother's nature.

Hey pay (A)ttention—here and now—to the way words sway

the play of swords in the calm talks of A sensai

then say messia Hu . . . r u or r u not? stop! rq not with the plotter's plot or the potter's pot

We are His seeds . . . woh how can we see as Hi as HE Hu ever
HE may B

Yo my bro how's it going? Well you know i'm flowin' from a well that's overflowing . . . working with family, friends toward the end of meeting for the ends to meet and become one as it always was and will be. I'm looking forward to speaking to you, and for words to show how happy I am to have heard from you. NEWayS what's new? ne new news? Is there anything new under the sun? Are there any new stars next to the moon? Or just what was there but now comes into VU because of being lifted from our daze due to shifting our gaze away from a Point to see more and others for they are all joined to the sky, as the sky is joined to the earth, and the earth to the Universe. Sepand jan soon enough is-here and now-here and now-is soon enough.

The present is the present-moment-the present is in the present tense

sense each sent, sent through you, to and for you to get through to you

then soon enough you will know when it is meant to Be.

SAAMI Say me: HOW's HE? HU u know DAD . . .

SHE OM o MOM and yourself your HEALTH
which is yOUR WEALTH

WELL WE'LL COME calm you aRe WELCOME where, where?

WE ARE where the WELL comes to be THE SAME=

# Addictions & Preferences

An addiction is any desire that makes one unhappy if it's not fulfilled

Life warns us to get rid of addictions every time we're uncomfortable

Addictions bring the user pleasures that are short-lived

and addicts worry about changes in life which make them feel less pleasureable

All of this keeps them out of the present of the here and now

We take a big step forward toward higher consciousness

the moment we become more fully aware how

much we pay for each addiction from the price of happiness

We are able to completely enjoy the same actions or experiences

when we uplevel the addiction to the status of a preference

because sooner or later addictions cause unhappiness

and when a preference is not satisfied we're indifferent for it was just a preference

# 2 Types of Power

In unreal power one defends

because there is an ego to be defended

Hence it is power over others

like that of kings, politicians, dictators

but they are hiding their impotence

The real religious, spiritual power of saints and prophets

is just simply pure power, not over others

Since it has no reference to the other, it prospers

it is very modest also so innocent

The power of mystics and sages is pre-eminent

that's why politics and religion are diametrically opposite

A politician can't be religious it's intrinsically impossible

and a religious person can't be a politician

for he is egoless, one with God and all creation

# Capitalism & Communism

Capitalism is the only natural system

it's a natural growth that hasn't been forced on any person

You know it's a natural phenomenon

which has grown out of freedom

so it's a part of human evolution

Capitalism is a democratic way of living

we're unequal because we're on different points of evolution

but equal opportunities need to be available for everyone

Communism in the name of equality destroys freedom

communism means to impose on others a system

It is the system that reduces everybody to the lowest denomination

it was shown to have taken away people's work incentive even slow their evolution

# Existentialism

At times I ask what's the recent reason I'm sent

My rhymes speak to represent the essence now present

Minding matters of the sole to be more whole

For finding answers to solve the whirling globe's woes

Foes oppose for they know not or supposedly forgot

That we're all one underneath these clothes, all is God

Nothing is lost where everything's source is found

Seeing sun and moon Pythagoras thought the Earth is round

Witnessing an apple drop Isaac Newton came across the law of gravity

Thomas Edison invented the method to store and use light: electricity

Alexander Fleming discovered bacteria-fighting penicillin

Observing fermentation Louis Pasteur founded pasteurization

These facts mentioned to your conscious' attention

To ask your conscience an obvious question:

Were these aforementioned men not profits?

Were they not a benefit to men who are God's subjects?

# Cognitivism

Cognitivism has two major components:

The first is methodological and the second one is theoretical

Methodologically it believes psychology, in principle,

can be fully explained by experiment, measurement and the scientific method

this is a reductionist goal believing that individual components

of mental function can be identified and meaningfully understood

Theoretically it believes that cognition consists of discrete internal mental states or symbols

whose manipulation can be described in terms of rules or algorithms

Cognitivism became psychology's dominant force in the late 20th century

replacing behaviorism as the most popular paradigm for understanding mental function

Main issues of interest for cognitive psychologists are the inner mechanisms of human thoughts

and the process of knowing, they've attempted to show the mental structures

that stand in a causal relationship to our physical actions

# Behaviorism

Also called the learning perspective is behaviorism

where any physical action is considered a behavior

A philosophy of psychology based on the proposition

upon which organisms act, think, feel or function

could and should be regarded as behaviors

that learning is defined as the acquisition of new behavior

There are two types of learning or conditioning

When a natural reflex responds to a stimulus is classic conditioning

like dogs salivate as they smell or see food Pavlov observed

Operant conditioning occurs when a response to a stimulus is reinforced

if reinforcement follows the stimulus' response,

then in the future becomes more probable the response

# Bio-Ecological Systems Theory

Specifies five types of nested environmental systems

with bi-directional influences within and between the systems

Urie Bronfenbrenner developed the theory

regarded as one of the leading scholars in developmental psychology

The microsystem are the immediate environments

family, school, peer group, neighborhood & childcare environments

The mesosystem is a system comprising connections between immediate environments

For example one's own home and school environments

The exosystem is external environmental settings which indirectly affect development

The macrosystem is the larger cultural context

national economy, subculture, political culture, and Eastern culture versus Western

and the Chronosystem is the life times patterning of transitions and environmental events

# Sociology

Is the systematic study of social

behavior and groups, focuses on the influence of social

relationships upon people's attitudes and behaviors

and on how the society establishes and changes

It's major objective is to identify underlying

recurring patterns of and influences on social behaviors

it goes beyond identifying patterns of social behavior

for such patterns it attempts to provide explanations

Sociologists examine the shared feelings and behaviors

of people within the larger social contexts of cultures, creeds, races or religions

The awareness of the relationship between individuals and the wider societies

is called the sociological imagination.

this awareness allows people to understand the relationship

between their immediate, personal, social settings

and their distant, impersonal social settings

that surrounds and helps to shape them

of the awareness an important element

is the ability to view one's own surroundings

as an outsider rather than from the limited perspective

of cultural biases and personal experiences

this awareness allows us to go beyond personal experiences

and observations to understand broader public issues

# Art, Music & Poetry

Art has to be a direct communication

between the artist's imagination

and that of the one looking or listening

Seeing creation as coming solely from imagination

art is it's clearest, nearest manifestation

The Creator is the Life, Life is creation

everything else is empty in comparison

And God created Music as the common language

so only poetry is the language that can manage

to reflect between Soul and Man any understanding

The consummate art of God between all poles of opposite expression

is poetry also known as rhythmic balanced interchanges

# Poets & Mystics

To religions love is the highest knowledge, scriptures were written in poetry, no coincidence

The significance is that it shows the affinity and closeness between poets and mystics

The difference is poets are mystics in some moments in which they have glimpses

A mystic is in the world of love and through the heart lives it

The poet sometimes falls down to the heart but goes to the head again

For some seconds the poet experiences reality but doesn't know the passage

The mystic living in the heart whatsoever he does becomes poetic

Mystics can't use prose because their prose is also poetic

# Many Metaphors and Some more Similes

i Be the dog walker, Sole's are GOD talkers

U know me the 1 wanter for all man, lands, and waters

Like silky Ricky slickly runnin' in the city

So all corners and fans are backed by brotherly love

Receiving wide passes from QT's for more TD's

Above grazed Mosses as easily as Randy does

The dandy Brandy tells a story of sweet candy love

And the Hennessy lends us the tendency to speak in many heavenly tongues

Verses crossin' overseas like Iverson conversin' for peace, cease-fire for all persons

Penned rhymes pouring in mikes when I recite the globe's goal of being more holy & right

The Light & Waves airing for the life and the way to be seen on screens

Hoping the media be assisting me like the Jazz's Stockton

For me to be scoring more all time points on networks

than Jordan did on B-ball courts with these spoken words

I've chosen to record taken many notes in life's classroom hearing the coach

I knew it was only a matter of time the spotlight's now mine to report

The news in my rap tunes . . . Yo Timbo, JDupri, D.R.E Pharrel of the neptunes

When can we link, get together, UNITe for real

I forgot to mention many like Primo of G.Starr who got mass appeal

I got dreams of marrying Guy-less queen/diva Madonna

And I want her to know I'm a Don P RIMA (Profit RimA)

Who has nothin' but love for all sides world-wide

Around from the front to the back, up down, left to the right for life

My heart beats art through arteries into vein cavities showing my pearly whites

Flowing to the live vibe riding the air waves I breath in the bright light is all I see

O High Life thou art my wife please let me know who else I need, you tell me!

# Carbon Jargon

Bet I hear copy cats

Yet I speak Godly raps

Gettin' high, wide and deep

Set my eyes on the prize, keep

Watching the light: inside is insight

Stopping time: outside is out of sight

Now sounds of the herd are unheard

Surrounding the suburb of the shepherd

Mountains abound our background

Fountains are around our flat's surrounds

Somewhere we're in the middle ground

Come where this center is found

Enter in and know the force

Rendered to show the source

Of course it glows from our core

On course to grow closer to the sole

# Don't Judge

Don't attempt to judge

unless you want to be judged

As they are, accept things

The technique for creating unity

to have a total existence within

stop opposing and attain silence, then begin

witnessing, simply observing, life as it is

don't interpret it only according to your views

# ForGive

When we don't forgive we believe

that retaliation against the people

who hurt us is just and justifiable

Anger expressed by punishing will not bring release

because the effect will hurt and anger others, the reason

there is a saying: "In forgiving there is a far greater pleasure

than in taking any form of revenge or vengeful measure

another reason to forgive the person who caused you pain

is to free yourself from the burden of hate

If the injury the other caused turns you into a hateful person

then the worst damage you've caused yourself not the other person

So to not hurt yourself in the process

and to not get in your own way of progress

you need to forgive to release the hurt

and to say that you no longer suffer

When we forgive we indicate that the pain is gone

and as you release it you are releasing the other person

We may choose never to speak to that person again

but what we really need is to feel free of the pain

# Giving & Taking

To many it seems a greater pleasure in taking

than there is in giving

But the pleasure that is had in giving

can never be found in taking

Whenever you've given, that giving has given you pleasure

and whenever you've taken, you've missed out on that pleasure

The more we're interested in taking then more thoughts will crowd the mind

If you understand it correctly, you'll see greed is mind

where there is no greed, there is meditation and charity

The scriptures say there's no greater sin than greed and no higher virtue than charity

The reason is that the charitable mind will become meditative

and when the day comes that you're ready to give

everything, seeking to gain nothing

then you will receive everything

# Caring Is Sharing

In the Garden was gained knowledge

and wisdom is attained in the forest

but it showers back down in the society

As ecstasy happens the care to share is there simultaneously

understand this we want to give that which we have

Increasing through sharing is whatever we have

So whatever you share does increase

sharing is the way that goes to increase

Now that you're aware of this and knowing

Sharing here is the formula for growing

# Real Man

It's very hard to meet a Real Man

since the world has become so fake

we're wearing masks to know our original face

we're trying to be happy by pretending happiness

we're trying to be loving by pretending lovingness

we're trying to be holy by pretending holiness

our so-called religions have been making us irreligious

the whole world is becoming full of false people

we are missing the ecstasy life can give to us

we are missing all that is good, beautiful and true

we have on many false faces so now who are you

# Up Close PersonA

Getting' up close & personal

to those who don't know me personally

I'm the he/she/it these parts of speech

come from the heart to be pardoning

Father forgiven to be Mother raised

now all I want to say are phrases that praise

All I gotta do here is get clearer

Can only be sincere when looking in a mirror

if we don't try on lie behind some disguise

For windows or doors to the sole are these eyes

so let them see cleaner, nearer

so existence's sea becomes neater

Good posture leads to heads getting' straight

to receive signs and signals make way

then veins and arteries can come closer to the heart of we

O sole, bless the five senses for life to be starting

and the sixth, even others unknown, enabling

us to be more able to know the unknowable

# A Bio

I'm an evolutionary child born during Iran's revolution. I was born September 24th 1979 in the U.S.A. Los Angeles, California is where I was raised. I came back to Iran when I was 10 or 11 years old and saw the after-effects of the Iran-Iraq war. Around that time I heard Run DMC, LL Cool J and rap. Not too long after that I started writing verses (or modern day poetry). My next door neighbor throughout these years was Richard Palmese C.E.O of Arista Records. In 1999, I was introduced to a DJ/producer and started recording. At that time my role model was eMineM and I was taking the music or art too literally. In the summer of 2000, I was driving under the influence and had an accident. Shortly after that I checked into Impact, a drug rehabilitation center. There I befriended the late Russell Jones a.k.a Ol' Dirty Bastard from the Wu-Tang Clan. In 2001, I decided to come back to Iran so I could get in touch with my roots and spend time with my family or foundation. In my family there are Prime Ministers. Prime Ministers of Education, Mayors, etc. Also there are are dervishes. I had the chance to be in the presence of dervishes. With the help of a dervish, who was my grandfather's student, I learned to read and understand the poetry of Persia's finest poets. Rumi, Hafez, Sa'adi, Ferdosi, Khayyam just to name a few. On my next trip, I visited their resting places. From there on out up to now the music's flowing. My songs are about unity, peace, freedom, love and awareness.